Work Smart and Succeed

Lessons and Examples on How to Succeed in Your Career

Jeff Rosenblum

Copyright © 2001 by Jeff Rosenblum

ISBN 0-7414-0634-9

Published by:

PUBLISHING.COM

Infinity Publishing.com
519 West Lancaster Avenue
Haverford, PA 19041-1413
Info@buybooksontheweb.com
www.buybooksontheweb.com
Toll-free (877) BUY BOOK
Local Phone (610) 520-2500
Fax (610) 519-0261

Printed in the United States of America

Printed on Recycled Paper

Published May, 2001

Dedication

This book is dedicated, first and foremost, to my parents. My mom, from the time I was born, tried to teach me right from wrong, and my dad introduced me to many of life's and work's greatest lessons, several of which appear within these pages.

Second, to the thousands of people with whom I have worked throughout my career and whose examples were the inspiration for this effort.

Acknowledgments

I would like to thank Pat Hadley-Miller, President of The Write Word, Inc., for her editorial proofreading service, and Infinity Publishing.com for helping me fulfill my dream of being a published author.

Introduction

As the title of this book, "Work Smart and Succeed," suggests, its goal is to provide you, the reader, with "Lessons and Examples on How to Succeed in Your Career." It is intended for everyone…no matter what your specific job, industry, or level of experience requires.

This book is the culmination of lessons I have learned throughout my more than twelve years working in the corporate world. It is also a compilation of examples based on the careers of about seventy people with whom I have worked during this time, although the situations and people's names mentioned in the examples are fictional.

In terms of my background, in 1988 I graduated from Syracuse University with a marketing degree and began my career working as an entry-level administrative assistant in a large advertising agency in New York City. I switched agencies a few times and, in the process, climbed my way up the ladder from middle management to vice president. I have also enjoyed success on the sales side of the advertising industry.

Over the course of this time, I have had the good fortune to work with thousands of interesting people as their peer, subordinate, manager, buyer, and seller. I have worked with people of all races, creeds, and colors, from all over the world; people from all sorts of backgrounds with different personalities; people with varying strengths and weaknesses.

This spectrum has always fascinated me because I have appreciated everyone's unique qualities. It has often been amazing for me to be part of a diverse group of people working together toward a common goal for the good of each other and the company. It has also been rewarding for me to be able to help others along the way by offering advice on how to get along with their coworkers and how to prosper in their jobs and careers.

Therefore, I have decided to share with a broader audience the lessons I have learned, including both what to do and what not to do in the workplace, which often applies to life in general. So with this in mind, please read on, and remember to work smart and succeed!

Lessons

Part I – People Skills

1. Know Who You Are 1
2. Everyone Is Different 3
3. Communication Is Key 5
4. Listen Carefully 7
5. Do Unto Others 9
6. Do Not Talk Behind Others' Backs 11
7. Offer Your Help To Others 13
8. Get Along With Everyone 15
9. Do Not Burn Any Bridges 17

Part II – It Is All In The Mind

10. Have A Positive Outlook 19
11. Be Passionate About Your Work 21
12. Keep Things In Perspective 23
13. Everyone Makes Mistakes 25
14. Be Flexible 27
15. The Goal Is To Learn 29
16. Think Before You Speak 31
17. Speak With Confidence 33
18. Sell Yourself 35

Part III – Subordinate To Manager

19. Pay Your Dues **37**
20. Be Patient, Your Time Will Come **39**
21. Manage Your Manager **41**
22. Expand Your Horizons **43**
23. Remember Where You Came From **45**
24. Treat Subordinates With Respect **47**
25. Do Not Yell At Others **49**
26. Delegate Whenever You Can **51**
27. How To Evaluate Others **53**

Part IV – Ready–Set–Go – Take Action

28. Honesty Is The Best Policy **55**
29. Never Complain **57**
30. Certain Topics Are A No-No **59**
31. Dress For Success **61**
32. Arrive On Time **63**
33. Prioritize And Juggle **65**
34. Double Check Everything **67**
35. A Time For Work And A Time For Play **69**
36. Take Breaks And Vacations To Avoid Burnout **71**

Part I – People Skills

1. Know Who You Are

A valuable thing to know in work, and in life, is who you are. Not who you want to be or who you wish you were but who you actually are deep down in your soul. You need to know what you believe in and what you stand for. You need to know your strengths and your weaknesses. With a complete and honest assessment of this information, you can firmly establish your goals.

Know Your Strengths
Everyone was born with a unique set of strengths, and it is vital to your success to be able to recognize yours. Some people are gifted physically, others mentally, and still others emotionally. Some people are naturally good with numbers, and others are better verbally. Some people are lucky to have a combination of several of these assets. By being aware of your strengths, you can work on developing them to help you succeed and achieve.

Know Your Weaknesses
Everyone also has weaknesses in one or more of these areas, so it is just as important to know your weaknesses as it is to know your strengths. In some cases, by working hard, weaknesses can be at least partially overcome. In other cases, natural weaknesses may prevail. Either way, by being cognizant of your shortcomings, you can develop a better sense of yourself and realize where you may or may not fit in.

Know Your Goals
A complete and honest assessment of your strengths and weaknesses will help you immeasurably with setting your goals. It will allow you to be aware of the tools you have, or

may not have, to help you find your way. An assessment will help you achieve a better understanding of yourself, where you want to go, and how you may be able to get there. It will give you direction and put you on a course armed with certainty and courage so you can achieve great things.

Examples
Stan entered the corporate world taking on projects requiring a high aptitude for mathematics, although working with numbers was not one of his strengths. Unaware of this, however, he rarely asked for help. Therefore, he made several critical mistakes early on that placed him on the wrong side of his managers. Eventually, Stan was let go by his company.

Katie entered the same company in the same position as Stan. She was aware that mathematics was not her strong suit, so she tried to concentrate the majority of her efforts on projects requiring more writing, which was one of her strengths. She did have to work with numbers from time to time, but knowing this was one of her weaker areas, she often asked for help. Katie parlayed her strengths, worked on her weaknesses, and quickly earned a promotion.

"Getting in touch with your true self must be your first priority." – Tom Hopkins, sales trainer and author.

2. Everyone Is Different

Just as important as knowing who you are is realizing that everyone is not the same as you. Everyone believes and stands for different things. Everyone has different strengths and different weaknesses. Therefore, everyone has different goals. To get along, you must realize, accept, and embrace other points of view. This is what makes work, and life, interesting. If everyone were the same as you, the world would be a boring place.

Everyone Has Different Strengths
While recognizing your own strengths is vital, it is just as critical to understand that other people may have different strengths. You cannot expect others to be as strong in certain areas as you are, just as others cannot expect you to be as strong in certain areas as they are. Knowing that everyone has varying degrees of strengths will help you work with others, help others, and learn from others in order to achieve your, and the company's, goals.

Everyone Has Different Weaknesses
You also have to recognize that just because you may be weak in certain areas, others may *not* be weak in these areas. To the contrary, some of your coworkers may be quite strong in these areas. These are the people you should go to when you need help, so you can try to strengthen your weaknesses. In turn, you should try to help others who are weaker in your areas of strength. This is what is known as teamwork. Teamwork helps you, helps others, and helps the company in general.

Everyone Has Different Goals
Since everyone has different strengths, and everyone has different weaknesses, it makes sense that everyone has different goals. Some people may want to concentrate their efforts in

one area, and others may set sail on an entirely different course. Goal setting is not a science. There is no right or wrong direction to follow. You have to set your own unique goals based on what you know you have to work with in order to achieve your ultimate desires.

Examples
Nancy was an intelligent young woman who entered the working world with high expectations. She had no problem completing her work in a rapid manner and expected everyone else to be able to do the same. Not everyone she worked with, however, was equally as gifted and, as a result, she came down hard on others. This did not sit well with those she worked with and for. Nancy did not last long in her company because she failed to realize that not everyone shared her same abilities.

Steve joined the same company as Nancy and was equally as intelligent. He quickly realized, however, not everyone he worked with was able to maintain his same pace. Therefore, he pitched in to help others around him and was looked upon as a team player and as a leader. This did not go unnoticed by his superiors, and Steve was rewarded with an early promotion.

"Most people can't understand how others can blow their noses differently than they do." – Ivan Turgenev (1818-1883), Russian novelist and short-story writer.

3. Communication Is Key

Effective communication is one of the keys to success in work and in life in general. People who can clearly express to others their thoughts, opinions, and ideas are way ahead of everyone else who cannot. People who are articulate are prime candidates for leadership positions in any company. The secret to good communication is to not just use your voice, but to utilize your body language as well.

Express Yourself Clearly
Expressing yourself clearly is the first step toward effective communication. This means when you have something to say, do not mumble. Do not swallow your words. Speak up, with confidence, so you will not only be heard, but you will be understood. Sure, you may know what you want to say, but the whole idea of communicating with others is that you want to let them hear, and comprehend, what you have to say.

Use Your Voice
Your voice is one of your communication tools. You should not speak too softly, because nobody will hear you, and you will have people saying, "What?" You should not speak too loudly either, because a loud voice might scare people. You should find a happy medium, and believe it or not, it takes practice. The same can be said for speaking too slowly or too quickly. Speak too slowly, and it will reflect either a lack of intelligence or timidity. Speak too quickly, and no-body will be able to follow along.

Use Your Body
Your body is another communication tool. The first thing you should do with your body when you speak with someone is make eye contact with that person. This radiates strength and confidence. Next, you should not just stand there limp

and let your voice do all of the talking. Put passion into your communication! Do not be afraid to use facial expressions, such as a smile or a frown, to help you express yourself. Also, there is nothing wrong with using your hands to help you make a point.

Examples

Chip was a smart young man and a hard worker. He was terrific with computers and was an excellent writer, but when it came to communicating with his coworkers, he lacked the most basic skills. First, he almost never looked people in their eyes when he spoke, which made him appear weak. Also, he did not speak clearly…he constantly mumbled and swallowed his words. Therefore, it did not matter how smart he was because nobody understood him. As a result, Chip's job did not last long.

Marc had a slight speech impediment that forced him to consciously monitor his communication with others. Therefore, when he spoke, he made sure to make eye contact. He also went out of his way to try to speak as clearly as possible so others could understand what he had to say. In addition, his facial expressions and hand gestures helped him radiate passion. Marc's tremendous efforts were clear for all to see, and he had no problem excelling in his career.

"To express the most difficult matters clearly and intelligently, is to strike coins out of pure gold." – Emanuel von Geibel (1815-1884), German poet.

4. Listen Carefully

The greatest communicators throughout history have been excellent listeners. There are times you can come off as a fantastic communicator, and an intelligent person, by simply listening and not even saying a word. Good listeners have enough patience to hear what others have to say, and then process the information they hear before they respond. This is not only how you communicate and work well with others, but it is also how you learn.

Communication Is A Two-Way Street

Many people feel that by speaking effectively they are good communicators, but this is not fully correct. Communication is a two-way street. This means that it takes at least two people to communicate effectively. When you speak, you are directing your words and your thoughts to at least one other person. After you speak, it is your time to listen. Do not think about what you just said or what you may want to say next. First listen, then think about how to respond, and then respond.

Everyone Wants To Be Heard

Just as you want people to listen to you when you speak, others want to be heard when they speak as well. Therefore, when other people are speaking to you, give them the same attention that you desire when you are speaking to them. Think about how you feel when people are listening to you. By being a good listener and really hearing what others have to say, you make them feel important by showing you care.

Listening Is The Key To Learning

Everyone has different and varying degrees of knowledge, so you can learn and gain knowledge from listening to other people. Whenever you listen to others, you put yourself in the position to learn something new. You may not learn something new every time, but you probably *will* learn more times than not. If you do not learn something new, you may gain reinforcement about something you already know. Either way, listening and learning will help you grow as an employee and as a person.

Examples
Theresa liked to speak to her coworkers but did not like to listen to them. With her, communication was a one-way street. As a result, she made her coworkers feel unimportant, and she looked bad in the process. She was a smart young woman and started her career off with a bang. Theresa's progress was stalled, however, because she did not learn new ways of approaching things, as she did not listen effectively.

Jada started at the bottom of the corporate ladder. She worked hard and learned a lot, mostly by asking questions and listening to others. She absorbed the information she learned as if she were a sponge. She also made others feel important because she listened to them, and everyone liked working with her. It was only a matter of time before others began looking to Jada for answers.

"Listening well is as powerful a means of communication and influence as to talk well." – John Marshall (1755-1835), American jurist and politician who served as the chief justice of the U.S. Supreme Court (1801-1835).

5. Do Unto Others

Do unto others as you would have done unto you. This means, regardless of the situation, treat others the same way you would like to be treated. If you are ever not sure what to do, say, or how to treat another person, always try to put yourself in the other person's shoes, and then act accordingly. This is the golden rule of work, and life, in general. Treat others with respect, and the respect will come back to you.

Golden Rule Of Life
Do unto others is the golden rule beyond just work but in life itself. If everyone lived by this one rule, the workplace, and the entire world, would be a much more peaceful, satisfying, and productive place. It seems as if this should be simple and should not even have to be explained, but it obviously is not. Things people do or say to each other and how people treat each other is clear proof that this is a rule that must constantly be reinforced.

Treat Others With Respect
Everyone deserves respect in the workplace. There are no exceptions. We all had to begin our career and pay some dues somewhere at sometime to get where we are now, whether we paid our dues in school or on the job training. Therefore, whether you are dealing with the president of your company or with an entry-level worker on his first day at the job, treat that person with nothing but respect.

The Respect Will Come Back To You
If you treat others with respect, the respect will come back to you. If you do not treat others with respect, you will not be respected. There is no more productive on-the-job relationship than one built from mutual respect. A relationship such as this will bode well for you, everyone around you, and the

company as a whole. Respect breeds respect. It is conta-gious, and there is no better place to start than by giving it.

Examples
Randy did not treat many people with respect. He constantly abused and talked down to people who came into his office in need of his services. This was embarrassing for him and all other parties involved. It provided for poor working re-lationships that hindered his, others, and his company's pro-ductivity. Therefore, he was not an employee for long. This all could have been avoided had Randy thought about how he would like to be treated and if he treated others accord-ingly.

Wayne, on the other hand, could not have been more pleas-ant to work with. After years of paying his dues as a re-spectful and respected employee, he had reached a senior level of management. Despite his position, he continued to treat others with the same respect he always had. Therefore, he continued to garner respect himself, and he kept on pro-gressing to the top of the company. The key to Wayne's suc-cess was that he always treated others the same way he al-ways wanted to be treated.

"Take the trouble to stop and think of the other person's feelings, his viewpoints, his desires and needs. Think more of what the other fel-low wants, and how he must feel." – Dr. Maxwell Maltz (1899-1975), author and creator of "Psycho-Cybernetics."

6. Do Not Talk Behind Others' Backs

One of the worst things you can do in work, and in life, is talk behind other people's backs. It is a selfish and cowardly act, and it is the quickest way to make enemies. Your comments will never fail to get back to those you are talking about, and the people you are talking to will want nothing to do with you. Bottom line, talking behind other people's backs will always come back to haunt you.

Quickest Way To Make Enemies
There is never a legitimate reason to talk behind other people's backs. If you do, you will gain a terrible reputation, and you will quickly make a lot of enemies. If you have something negative to say about someone, be a stand-up person, and say it to that person only. That person can, and will, respect you for it. It will also help clear the air and most likely lead to a mutual understanding that will serve to help your relationship with that person and benefit the company overall.

Your Comments Will Always Get Back To Them
If you talk behind other people's backs, your comments will never fail to get back to those you are talking about. You may think you will get away with it, but words spread rapidly in the workplace. If people know you are someone who talks about others behind their backs, they will begin to talk about you behind your back. What they will surely talk about is the negative comments you made about others.

Others Will Want Nothing To Do With You
You may think, by talking behind other people's backs, it will hurt the people you are talking about. You may even believe you will get some laughs and make some friends because of it. You could not be more wrong. You will only hurt yourself, people will laugh *at* you not with you, and you

will lose whatever friends you may have because they will never believe that you are not talking about *them* behind their backs.

Examples
Julie had a bad habit of constantly talking about other people behind their backs. She seemed to have a lot of people willing to listen to her, and she even generated some laughter as a result of her nasty comments. When she left the room, however, she became the subject of the talk and the laughter. More often than not, the people she spoke about were quickly in on it, and she was resented. Julie was also soon fired.

Janet was bright, articulate, and exuded confidence. She expected a lot from the people who worked for her, and she was often firm and direct. If she had a problem with someone, she spoke to that person only, face-to-face. Many people who did not work for her thought she was too tough, demanding, and must be difficult to work for. The people who worked for her, however, could not feel more differently. She was well liked, respected, and always fair. Janet quickly rose to the top of her company.

"I do not speak of what I cannot praise." – Johann Wolfgang von Goethe (1749-1832), German poet, dramatist, novelist, and scientist.

7. Offer Your Help To Others

One of the greatest ways to help yourself at work, and in life, is to offer your help to others. Helping others will make you feel good just as it will help those you are helping feel good. It is the quickest way to make allies not only of those you are helping, but also of those around you who will see you as someone they can turn to when they need help themselves. It will establish you in your company as a team player and as a leader, one whom everyone else will want to work with and for.

Quickest Way To Make Allies
Offering your help to others is the quickest way to make allies, and you can never have too many allies at work. Those people you help will, naturally, be your allies. In addition, when others see you are the type of person willing to help those who need it, they will like, respect, help, and support you when you need it. Everyone, no matter how experienced, established, or talented, will require help somewhere along the way. It is comforting to know that help is always near.

Will Establish You As A Team Player
Offering your help to others will establish you as a team player in your company. Everyone wants a team player on his team. When everyone wants you on his team, you provide yourself with the ultimate security in your company. Jobs change quickly, so the position you are in today may not be necessary tomorrow. If you are known as a team player, if something happens to your job, there will always be others who will want you to play a role on their team.

Will Establish You As A Leader
Offering your help to others will establish you as a leader. Everyone wants to promote a leader, because everyone wants

to work for a leader. Leaders are hard to find because most people are followers. Those who can single themselves out as leaders will be on the fast track in their companies. Just remember as you move up the corporate ladder, helping others is what helped you succeed, so never stop offering your help to others no matter how high you climb.

Examples
Peter was fairly intelligent, but he was concerned about his work and his work only. He did not offer his help to others nor did he ask for much help from others. As a result, he was not considered a team player, and he did not show leadership material. Peter was regularly bypassed when plum job assignments and promotions came up, so he soon became disgruntled and left the company.

Veronica worked at the same company but could not be more different than Peter. She was of average intelligence but worked hard. While she was always busy with her own work, she consistently offered to pitch in to help others. Helping others made her feel good, allowed her to learn more, and gave her exposure to upper management. When she needed help, she asked, and there was always plenty available to her. Veronica was considered a team player, a leader, and rapidly advanced.

"It is one of the beautiful compensations of this life that no one can sincerely try to help another without helping himself." – Charles Dudley Warner (1829-1900), American writer and editor.

8. Get Along With Everyone

The quickest way to climb up the corporate ladder is to get along with everyone you work with. You do not have to be best friends with everyone at work, but you should be able to get along with everyone. It has already been established that everyone is different, with varying strengths, weaknesses, and goals. By showing you can get along with everyone, you will inherit the reputation of a versatile employee able to work with different people in a multitude of situations. There is no stopping someone with this trait.

Quickest Way To Move Up The Corporate Ladder

When upper management looks to promote one of their employees, among the most important criteria they look for is someone who can work with a diverse group of people in various situations. Because, after all, in addition to a position with greater responsibility, that is what a promotion is. Upper management often looks for someone who can step into a new environment and be able to work with everyone they come into contact with. Not everyone can do this. If you can, you will stand out from the crowd.

Do Not Have To Be Best Friends With Everyone

Getting along with everyone does not mean you have to be best friends with everyone. To the contrary, some of the best employees are not those who are best friends with everyone, but those who have solid, professional working relationships with everyone. Because everyone is different, being best friends with everyone is nearly impossible and simply not necessary. Being able to work with everyone, however, is a tremendous asset.

Should Be Able To Work With Everyone

Since everyone is different in the workplace, personalities often clash. When this happens, if not handled swiftly and properly, the employees', and the company's productivity suffers. If these personality clashes can be avoided before they begin to take shape, the employees', and the company's productivity will thrive. The way to avoid these personality clashes, and the negative results on productivity, is to be open-minded and be able to work with everyone.

Examples
Ned was a smart, affable, and free-spirited young man when he entered the corporate world. He soon warmed to everyone and seemed to make friends quickly. When it came to getting work done, however, especially when having to deal with others a bit different and more serious than him, he ran into problems. He chose only to see things his way and work at his own pace regardless of deadlines. Ned did not last long in the corporate world.

Jessie, on the other hand, thrived in a corporate environment. Similar to Ned, she was amiable, but she was not looking to be best friends with everyone. She was just hoping to establish good working relationships so she could perform her job well. She succeeded and got along with everyone. Others helped her, and she helped them. This did not go unnoticed, and Jessie was soon promoted.

"People have been known to achieve more as a result of working with others than against them." – Dr. Allan Fromme (1915-), psychologist, lecturer, and author.

9. Do Not Burn Any Bridges

The last thing you want to do in the business world is burn any bridges, or make any enemies, because the business world is way too small. Sooner or later, "burned bridges" will come back to haunt you, often when you least expect it. You never know where you will be tomorrow – you may need to "cross" that bridge you burned. Also, you never know where others will be tomorrow, so be careful not to make any enemies.

The Business World Is Way Too Small

As Walt Disney's theme states, "it's a small world after all," so imagine how small the business world is. If you put in enough time in business, it will seem as if everyone knows everyone else or at least has some connection to each other. This can be a good and comfortable thing, if you do not burn any bridges. If you do burn bridges, however, they will usually come back to burn you.

You Never Know Where You Will Be Tomorrow

The business world is transient, so you never know where you will be tomorrow. If something happens to your job, or you simply desire a change, you will have to search for another job. Potential employers often inquire about you to others you once worked with. If a potential employer gets in touch with one of your allies, you will be fine. If you burned any bridges, however, and the potential employer finds them, you will be at the burned bridges' mercy. You can be sure this is not a place you want to be.

You Never Know Where Others Will Be Tomorrow

Let us say you once worked with someone you simply did not like. Your working relationship ended as you or she either moved on to another position or left to go to another company. You said some nasty things because you did not think you would ever have to deal with that person again. You burned a bridge. Years pass, you are in another company, and low and behold, look who joins your new company, the bridge you once burned, and she is now your boss. Burned bridges are a big mistake!

Examples
Eric once worked at a company for a manager who was well known in her industry for being tough but fair. The two did not see eye to eye, so he soon obtained another job. Upon leaving the company, he said some harsh things to his then boss. He burned a bridge. After several months at his new company, he found out about the job opening of his dreams. The manager at this dream job, however, knew his ex-boss and did some checking. Eric did not get his dream job because of the bridge he once burned.

Joe worked at the same company for the same manager as Eric. Similarly, he did not always agree with her, and he often confronted her, but in a dignified and professional manner. Eventually, he made a lateral move into another group, and the two parted with mutual respect for each other. When his dream job opening presented itself, his dream job manager knew his ex-boss, too. He did some checking, and Joe ended up getting his dream job.

"The destruction of the past is perhaps the greatest of all crimes." – Simone Weil (1909-1943), French social philosopher and political activist.

Part II – It Is All In The Mind

10. Have A Positive Outlook

It is always important to come into work with a positive outlook and maintain that disposition throughout the day. It is inevitable, as the day progresses, you will be faced with many challenging situations and circumstances, and things always look better when the glass is half full. In addition, if you have a positive outlook, others will be drawn to you, and your positive energy will be infectious.

<u>Things Always Look Better When The Glass Is Half Full</u>
You have two choices of how to view any given situation or circumstance at work or in life. You can look at things in a positive light, as the glass being half full. Or, you can look at things in a negative light, as the glass being half empty. Things always look better when the glass is half full. This means, by looking at things in a positive light, you automatically feel better and deal with a given situation or circumstance with a much clearer head.

<u>People Want To Be Around Positive People</u>
Most people prefer to be around positive people rather than around negative people. Everyone wants to feel better about themselves and the situations or circumstances they have to deal with. People are inspired and uplifted just by being around and working with positive people. As a result, productivity on the job usually bears fruit. On the other hand, people are uninspired and deflated just by being around and working with negative people. As a result, productivity on the job normally suffers.

<u>Your Positive Attitude Will Rub Off On Others</u>
Positive attitude is contagious. If you come into work with a positive outlook, your coworkers will most likely catch it.

There is no more satisfying or more productive office environment than a group of positive people working with each other toward a common set of goals. In addition, your inflection of positive energy on others will show, and you will be regarded as a leader with the outstanding trait of being able to motivate others.

Examples
Gerald came to the office every day with a negative attitude. He had a frown on his face and dreaded his work even before he started. As a result, he alienated his coworkers. Nobody liked working with him, and he was never considered for a promotion for fear that his negative aura would spread. Gerald was quickly terminated.

Winona had the same position in the same company as Gerald, but she was always smiling, and made the most of what her job entailed. Her positive outlook quickly spread to her coworkers who all enjoyed working with her. Winona was looked upon as a leader and soon moved on to bigger and better things within the company.

"A positive attitude can really make dreams come true – it did for me." – Zina Garrison, former professional tennis player.

11. Be Passionate About Your Work

In life, you always get in direct proportion to what you give. The same is true in work. If you put passion behind your work, you will be justly rewarded. If you are going to do a job, you may as well do it the best you can. Show your co-workers that you care about what you do by putting all of your heart and soul into it. Always strive for the best results, and remember to take pride in your accomplishments.

Show That You Care About What You Do
If you take pride in your work and show that you care about what you do, the results will be reflected accordingly, and people will stand up and take notice. In contrast, if you are indifferent toward your job and are careless regarding your work, that will show, and others will be sure to take note. Those who care about their work are the ones who move onward and upward, and those who do not care are the ones who get left behind.

Always Strive For The Best Results
By being passionate about your work and showing that you care about what you do, you set yourself up to achieve the best results. In a corporate setting, results are often the bottom line and the main criteria for how workers are judged. Results are what rewards such as salary, bonuses, and promotions are usually based upon. Always remember that results do not just come to some by chance. Results come to those who put their blood, sweat, and tears behind their work.

Take Pride In Your Accomplishments
When you achieve the results you are striving for, do not be afraid to take pride in your accomplishments, but never rub your achievements in your coworkers' faces by showing off or bragging. Taking pride in your accomplishments means

feeling good about what you have achieved. Allow yourself time to enjoy the fruits of your labor. Just do not develop a big head over it. Most importantly, use your accomplishments to motivate yourself to continue to move forward and strive for even greater success.

Examples

Cara was an intelligent young woman when she began her career, but from the start, her coworkers could tell she did not like her job. Actually, she said it herself on a regular basis. She lacked passion for her work. She simply did not care about what she did or the results she achieved. She did not take pride in anything she might have accomplished. Therefore, Cara's career did not last long.

Harry started at the same company shortly before Cara, but unlike her, he rose up the ranks quickly. From his earliest days on the job, the passion he exuded for his work was apparent. He cared about everything he did, and his results showed. While he took great pride in his accomplishments, he was respectful and diplomatic at the same time. Over the years, as Harry received one promotion after the other, he never lost his passion and always strove for greater success.

"I don't think I can play any other way but all out. I enjoy the game so much because I'm putting so much into it." – George Brett, former Major League Baseball player, now a member of the National Baseball Hall of Fame.

12. Keep Things In Perspective

No matter what happens throughout your career, always keep things in perspective. Although work is important, unless you are a doctor or in a similar profession, work is not life or death. You must always maintain balance by having a life consisting of other people and interests outside of work. Also, as you practice this in your own life, keep it in mind when dealing with other people at work.

<u>Work Is Important, But It Is Not Life Or Death</u>
Only a few people hold life and death in their hands when they are at their job. For the majority of others, although work is something to take seriously, it must be kept in its proper perspective. Throughout your career, with absolute certainty, you will have to handle a multitude of problems and mishaps that will occur. Some of them will even be a direct fault of yours or of others you work with. During these times, you have to step back, take a deep breath, and remember it is work, not life or death.

<u>Maintain Balance In Your Life</u>
Work should not be all you do. Coworkers should not be the only people you do things with. Bottom line, your work should not be your entire life, and your entire life should not revolve around your job. If it does, then you will quickly burn out and turn into a workaholic. Then, not only will you have no personal life, but your professional life will dramatically suffer as well. It is vital to maintain a balanced lifestyle consisting of activities, interests, family, and friends you can enjoy outside of your job.

<u>Remember This When Dealing With Others</u>
When it comes to dealing with others at work, remember they have lives on the outside too, so manage your expectations accordingly. While it is important that you and every-

one you work with be dedicated to your job, everyone's health and families take precedence. Personal emergencies will arise, sometimes at the most inopportune times. Therefore, you should be understanding, empathetic, and flexible in these situations.

Examples
Carla joined her company and immediately impressed management by her hard work and dedication. Therefore, she earned a couple of quick promotions. Soon, however, she began to take her job too seriously. She eliminated practically everything else in her life, logged in long hours, and took work home with her on a regular basis. She expected everyone else to as well. Not long into this workaholic lifestyle did she begin to make consistent mistakes and feel ill. Carla eventually burned out and left her job.

Terry worked at a similar company to Carla and was also quickly promoted a couple of times. He maintained the same hard work ethic in his new positions as he did in his previous ones. Simultaneously, he married, had children, and enjoyed a variety of sports and leisure activities with his family and friends. He encouraged his coworkers to do the same, and they greatly appreciated him for it. Terry has continued to flourish in both his career and his life.

"Rule #1: Don't sweat the small stuff. Rule #2: It's all small stuff." – Dr. Michael R. Mantell, psychologist, author, television, radio, and print personality.

13. Everyone Makes Mistakes

From the beginning of your career until the end of it, you will make an infinite number of mistakes. Everyone will. Everyone does. Everyone has. Nobody wants to make them, they just do. There is simply no getting around them because everyone is human. You should try to minimize the frequency of your mistakes, but when you make mistakes, it is how you deal with them that counts. The key is to learn from your mistakes, and try not to repeat the same ones.

Mistakes Are Inevitable
The sooner you realize mistakes are inevitable, for you and everyone else you work with, the better off you and everyone else you work with will be. Once you realize this, you should still try to do things correctly, but when mistakes occur, you will not get overly angry, frustrated, or upset. You will simply deal with the mistakes in a calm and rational manner.

It Is How You Deal With Your Mistakes That Counts
Dealing with mistakes in a calm and rational manner will serve you and everyone else you work with best. This means that when mistakes occur, first recognize a mistake was made, admit it if it was your fault, and either forgive yourself or the other person, or people, at fault. Then, try to figure out how the mistake happened, and try to correct it. If another mistake occurs, just start again from the beginning of this process.

Try Not To Make The Same Mistakes More Than Once
You can learn more from your mistakes than from things you do correctly right off the bat. The key lesson discovered from mistakes is to learn as much as you can from them so the same mistakes will be less likely to occur in the future. If you try not to make the same mistakes more than once,

you will get better at your job as you put in more time and gain more experience.

Examples
Frank joined the corporate world and expected to get ahead easily. He carelessly breezed through the initial projects he was assigned and, as a result, made numerous mistakes. When these errors were pointed out to him, he often became agitated and blamed others or extraneous circumstances. He rarely accepted responsibility for his own mistakes, so he was unable to learn from them and usually repeated the same errors again and again. Therefore, Frank failed to grow as an employee and was soon fired.

Evan entered into a similar corporate environment as Frank. His initial assignments proved to be somewhat difficult for him, so he made several mistakes. He appreciated being made aware of these errors and tried as hard as he could to learn from them in order to avoid making the same mistakes on future assignments. His managers continued to give him more work, and in time, his mistakes appeared less frequently. Evan soon became an outstanding employee and was promoted right on schedule.

"The successful man will profit from his mistakes and try again in a different way." – Dale Carnegie (1888-1955), American self-improvement educator and author.

14. Be Flexible

The most valuable employees in the workplace are often those who are the most flexible with their time, skills, and willingness to tackle new tasks. In today's constantly changing business culture, with all of the enhanced technology that comes along with it, it is critical to be prepared for any situation. New and advanced ways of doing things are being developed every day, so you must constantly learn to adjust. You should also be ready to improvise, as you will often have to make spontaneous decisions.

Be Prepared For Any Situation
In order to be prepared for any situation that may occur at work, first it is necessary to have an open mind. If your mind is closed, you will not be willing or able to accept something different. Then, you must be armed with a flexible time schedule, job skills, and an eagerness to take on new challenges. With all of these weapons in your arsenal, you will position yourself as a valued and versatile employee.

Learn To Adjust
If you are used to doing things one way, and you are forced to change and do things another way, you must be able to learn to adjust or else you will be left behind. In order to be able to learn to adjust and be prepared for change, it is helpful to keep yourself abreast of the latest technology. It is also beneficial to be aware of current news and events that shape your industry.

Learn To Improvise
There will be times at work when you will be forced to improvise and think on your feet. Being up to date on the latest technology, as well as being cognizant of your industry's current news and events, will help in these situations, too. If you are as prepared as anyone else, have confidence in your

ability to make spontaneous decisions. Sometimes you may even have to take risks. Improvising is a skill that can be developed the more it is practiced; so do not be afraid of doing it.

Examples

Leroy had several years of experience in his industry when new technology started being introduced at a rapid rate. He had been doing his job the same way throughout his career, so he was not eager to embrace change. Shortly, many of his coworkers with far less experience than he had began passing him by with their skills. He continued to resist change, and he fell further behind. Eventually, Leroy was unable to keep up with the efficiency of his coworkers, and he was soon out of a job.

Paula was in the same position at the same company as Leroy. She also had a few years on the job behind her and was used to working in a certain manner. When new technology was introduced she, too, was a bit skeptical, but she kept an open mind and decided to give it a try. Although this new technology initially forced her to take a few steps back, she was aware of the potential it had to help her grow. She did grow and soon began teaching and helping others. Paula was promoted shortly thereafter.

"We must make the best of those ills which cannot be avoided." – Alexander Hamilton (1755-1804), American politician who was the first U.S. secretary of the treasury (1789-1795).

15. The Goal Is To Learn

The ultimate goal you can set every day of work is to learn. The surefire way to learn is by asking questions. There is always someone at work you can ask questions of and learn from, and you can always learn something new. Learning is what keeps your job, and your life, interesting. When you learn, you grow as an employee and as a person in general. It does not get much more fulfilling than that.

<u>Ask Questions</u>
By asking questions at work, you will put yourself in a position to learn. The more you learn, the more knowledge you will gain about your job. The more knowledge you gain about your job, the more apt you will be to advance in your company. The more you advance in your company, the more exposure you will receive. The more exposure you receive, the more questions you will be able to ask, and the upward cycle of your career path will continue.

<u>You Can Always Learn Something</u>
You can always learn something at work, whether it is about your job, your company, or your industry. In addition to learning from your coworkers by asking questions, you can also learn from books, magazines, trade journals, and the Internet. Sometimes, the best way to learn is by doing. Accept new challenges, expand your horizons, and there is no telling how much you will learn.

<u>Learning Is Growing</u>
If you want to grow as an employee and as a person in general, you must continually learn. The day you stop learning is the day you will stop growing. The day you stop growing is the day you should look to do something new. When you do not grow, you stagnate, and you waste your time and everyone else's time around you. Do not waste your life.

Whether you ask questions, read, surf the Web, or use a combination of all three, enjoy the process of learning and growing.

Examples
Jennifer began her career, and her main objective from day one was to get her immediate assignments done without asking many questions and with no regard to learning about her new job, company, or industry. At first, she was able to get by, but over time, her lack of curiosity caught up with her, and she did not progress at the same pace as her peers. Jennifer failed to learn as much as her peers, and as a result, she did not grow at the same rate.

Emma started on the same career path as Jennifer, but she had a burgeoning curiosity. She was constantly picking her coworkers' brains with the goal of learning as much as she could. She also read anything and everything related to her profession with the same intention in mind. Emma quickly became a rising star at the company and never stopped trying to learn more along the way.

"Develop a passion for learning. If you do, you will never cease to grow." – Anthony J. D'Angelo, author.

16. Think Before You Speak

If you gather your thoughts and think about what you want to say before you actually say it, what you end up saying will be wiser and more appropriate. People often do not think, however. They say the wrong thing at the most inopportune time and regret saying it later. The words people speak have implications. They can either help or hurt. Therefore, make sure your choice of words and timing is right, and do not speak just to hear yourself speak. Speak with a specific purpose in mind.

<u>Gather Your Thoughts</u>
The first step in speaking with a purpose is to gather your thoughts. Since work can often be a fast-paced, frenetic environment, you may have several things you are doing or thinking about at the same time. Therefore, when it is your turn to speak, either in response to another or to initiate dialog, think about what you want to say before you actually say it. Keep in mind that gathering your thoughts should not be a long process. It should be instantaneous, so others should not even be aware you are doing it.

<u>Make Sure Your Timing Is Right</u>
Once you know what you want to ask or say, make sure your timing is right. Of course, if you are asked a question, usually the timing is right to respond. This point applies more to when you decide to ask a question or begin a conversation. Think about whether it is the appropriate time and place to ask or say something. If it is, after you have gathered your thoughts, then go for it. If not, wait for a better situation.

<u>Do Not Speak Just To Hear Yourself Speak</u>
It is important to note that gathering your thoughts and making sure your timing is right to speak does not mean being afraid to ask or say what you want. To the contrary, you

should never be afraid to ask questions and speak your mind, but you should always do it in the most thoughtful and constructive way. Do not haphazardly speak just to hear yourself speak. This means, do not speak simply because you may feel you have not spoken in a while. These are the times you may say things you may regret later.

Examples

Jake was a smart and gregarious young man. He worked in a small group that was part of a much larger company. Initially, the others in his group enjoyed his outgoing nature and sense of humor. As time went by, however, he turned a lot of them off because he never stopped talking, usually about nothing noteworthy. It seemed as if he just liked to hear the sound of his voice. Eventually, he began saying more of the wrong things at more of the wrong times. Jake was soon ousted from his group.

Alan was employed in the same company as Jake, but he worked in a different small group. He was also bright, sociable, and humorous, but he was thoughtful and sensitive at the same time. He did not just say anything that popped into his head because he was aware that words often have an impact on other people. Instead, he chose the most appropriate times for his questions, comments, suggestions, and jokes. Alan quickly became one of the more popular members of his group.

**"Talking without thinking is like shooting without taking aim." —
Proverb**

17. Speak With Confidence

Once you decide you have something to say, do not be shy about it. Give it everything you have, and say it with confidence. If you speak with confidence, people will believe you know what you are talking about. If you are timid about it, others will feel uneasy and unsure about what you are saying. Always be aware, however, that there is a fine line between confidence and arrogance. You always want to show confidence, but you never want to appear arrogant.

<u>When You Say Something, Say It With Confidence</u>
When you have something to say, you have a choice of how to communicate it. Together with your actual words, this choice dictates how you will be perceived, and perception is often reality. Either you can express yourself with confidence and appear strong, or you can exhibit apprehension and seem weak. The choice is yours. Just remember, in the workplace, as in life, confidence and strength will carry you a long way. Apprehension and weakness will get you nowhere.

<u>People Will Believe What You Are Saying</u>
When you have something to say, and you decide to say it, you want people to believe it. When you speak with confidence, people are far more likely to believe what you are saying than when you speak with apprehension. When you speak with confidence, and people believe what you are saying, you will be looked upon as a leader in your company. The business world is always searching for leaders.

<u>There Is A Fine Line Between Confidence And Arrogance</u>
As advantageous as it is to be confident, it is not advantageous to appear arrogant, and you must always walk the fine line between the two. When you exude confidence, you radiate strength, people have faith in you, and you display

leadership qualities. When you come off as arrogant, how-ever, people perceive you as obnoxious, egotistical, and con-ceited. These are not the qualities you want to have in the corporate world because it could lead to an untimely exit.

Examples
Stacy was an educated and qualified young woman who worked for a large company. She was a hard worker and dedicated to her job, but she lacked confidence when it came to making decisions and answering questions from her co-workers. Although she usually knew the proper things to do and frequently had correct answers, she was shy about ex-pressing them. Therefore, her coworkers began losing faith in Stacy, and she never fulfilled her potential.

Robyn was also a capable young woman who had a job in a similar size company as Stacy. She was knowledgeable as well, but her main strength was her aura of confidence. Her motto was, "If something is worth saying, it is worth saying with confidence." Therefore, her coworkers often looked to her for direction. As a result, Robyn distinguished herself as a leader, and that is just what she became.

"Be still when you have nothing to say; when genuine passion moves you, say what you've got to say, and say it hot." – David Herbert (D. H.) Lawrence (1885-1930), English novelist, playwright, poet, and artist.

18. Sell Yourself

Even if your official occupation is not sales, you are a salesperson, because you are always selling yourself. No matter what it is you do, you are constantly selling your ideas, opinions, and creations to others...maybe not for monetary value, but for other rewards such as approval, agreement, and encouragement. If you can be successful selling yourself, you have the ability to sell anything, and a good salesperson will always be successful.

You Are Always Selling Yourself

As soon as you wake up in the morning and get dressed, you are beginning to sell yourself. It is part of the package you present to the world when trying to gain acceptance. At work, when your input is requested, you are being called upon to sell your thoughts, suggestions, and recommendations to your coworkers with the goal of winning supporters. There is simply no way around it. Like it or not, you are always selling yourself.

If You Can Sell Yourself, You Can Sell Anything

If you become proficient at selling yourself, there will be no stopping you in this world, and you will be able to sell anything. If you can combine your appearance, personality, and intellectual ability into a seamless force, you will put yourself at a tremendous advantage when called upon to sell or to lead. To do this well takes time and effort and often requires continuous trial and error.

A Good Salesperson Will Always Be Successful

If you become a good salesperson, you will be a hot commodity in the business world. Not everyone has the ability and the intestinal fortitude to sell. That is why those who do, and do it well, are traditionally highly regarded and rewarded in their companies. Once you prove that you can be successful at selling, you can often pick and choose where and how you would like to spend your career. In addition, you can often play a significant role in determining how much money you will make.

Examples
Martin was a good entry-level employee in his company. He was given several tasks and had few problems completing them. When he was promoted, he was called upon more frequently to offer his ideas and opinions, but he had a difficult time selling his thoughts and suggestions to others. He did not take the time to work on his presentation and it showed. Surprisingly to his coworkers, he left his company to try his hand at an actual sales job. As they expected, Martin did not succeed.

Sean also started at the bottom of a similar company to Martin's. He, too, performed well early on and earned a promotion. As his input was more often requested, he seized the opportunities and, through trial and error, began offering his opinions and recommendations in a well thought out manner. He reveled in his ability to sell his ideas successfully. Sean found his niche and is now a top salesman.

"Everyone lives by selling something." – Robert Louis Stevenson (1850-1894), Scottish novelist, essayist, and poet.

Part III – Subordinate To Manager

19. Pay Your Dues

Everyone had to pay "dues" at one time or another, and you either had to, or will have to, as well. Paying your dues means starting at the bottom of a company and climbing your way up through a combination of hard work, dedication, and perseverance. When you start at the bottom of a company, you should make it your duty to accept any and all tasks because nothing is too small or beneath you. Most importantly, excel at those tasks.

Start At The Bottom
The bottom is the best place to begin your career for a couple of reasons. First, there is nowhere to go but up. Second, and the more important reason, is that you have the opportunity to absorb and learn everything, every step of the way. This will prove to be most valuable to you as you work your way up the ranks. Also, as you are striving to get to the top, always remember where you came from.

Accept All Tasks
The quickest way to begin your ascent to the top is to accept, and volunteer for, every assignment possible during your time at the bottom. By doing this, you will not only put yourself in a position to learn as much as you can, but you will be able to prove yourself in the most timely fashion. Do not feel you are above, or too big, for any task because you are not. Anything that comes your way at the bottom, just do it!

Excel At All Tasks
It is vital to excel at all tasks when you are at the bottom even if, and especially *if*, the tasks are as simple as filing, making copies, or typing letters. Once you prove you can do

these things, you will be given more responsible assignments. If you take these basic tasks too lightly, it will take much longer for you to be able to move on to bigger and better projects.

Examples
Paul was a bright and ambitious young man who obtained an entry-level position within a company right out of college. During his first few days, he was disappointed because he was being asked to do things he thought were beneath him and a waste of his time such as proofreading letters and distributing memos. His dissatisfaction showed as he grew complacent and bitter. Paul did not give himself enough time to get past this stage, and he quickly left the company.

Marla started at the bottom of the same company as Paul, also directly after college. Fortunately, her future manager offered her some prophetic advice upon hiring her. The advice was, the sooner she could show she could perform the most basic tasks, the quicker she would be given more responsible assignments. She took this to heart and enthusiastically accepted and excelled at everything that was thrown her way. She even volunteered for more. Marla moved up fast, and she is now part of upper management.

"Show me a man who cannot bother to do little things and I'll show you a man who cannot be trusted to do big things." – Lawrence Dale Bell (1894-1956), aircraft designer who founded Bell Aircraft Corp., which later became Bell Aerospace.

20. Be Patient, Your Time Will Come

It is natural to begin at an entry-level position in a company and want to move up right away. There is nothing wrong with this...it is called ambition...but it does not always work this way. Actually, sometimes it is better if it does not, because you will have more time to learn and gain a certain comfort level within your company. It is important to be patient, because your time will come. You have to make the most at each level, and soon enough, your hard work will pay off. Eventually, the cream rises to the top.

Savor Your Time At Each Level
In your career, you will probably do only one stint at the bottom. The same goes for each step after that. Therefore, you may as well savor your time at each level. This means, take advantage of what each position from bottom to top has to offer, from the things you learn to the people you meet. If you do, when you become a manager, you will be fully aware of what is required at each step and you will have no problem relating to, and managing, your subordinates at each level. This bottom to top experience is priceless.

Your Hard Work Will Be Noticed
At times it may seem as if you are working hard and nobody is taking notice. People probably are, because it is difficult not to take note of someone putting in hard work. Even if they are not, however, just keep plugging away, because sooner or later people will. Sometimes it will be when you least expect it. When they do take notice, it will be worth it, because hard work is ultimately rewarded.

Eventually, The Cream Rises
In the business world, just as in a cup of coffee, eventually, the cream rises, and it rises to the top. This means that if you are a hard working, dedicated team player and leader, sooner

or later you will separate yourself from the rest, and you will gravitate toward the height of your company. Just remember to never give up. It will only be a matter of time until you are in a position to reap the rewards of your success.

Examples

Mara was hired into an entry-level position just out of college. She was a smart, amiable, and determined young woman who worked hard. She noticed one of her coworkers, who began at her company shortly before she did, get a quick promotion. Although her coworker was fortunate to be in the right place at the right time, Mara felt she should be promoted soon after. Unfortunately, a spot was not open when she had expected, so she grew resentful, left the company, and never gave herself a chance.

Brad had also recently graduated from college when he began at the bottom of the same company as Mara. He was a young man with a good attitude. He dedicated himself to doing the best job he could in order to move up the corporate ladder, but he soon saw others getting promoted before him. Undeterred, he kept plugging away and learning all he could as he felt his time had to come soon. Brad's patience paid off as he earned a promotion, became a great manager, and was promoted again.

"Our patience will achieve more than our force." – Edmund Burke (1729-1797), Irish-born British politician and writer.

21. Manage Your Manager

Just as your manager manages you, you have to learn how to manage your manager. This means that you have to learn how your manager works and how you can best work with him, so you can share a productive relationship. Start by taking note of your manager's style, because all managers are different. Then, test your manager's limits, but make sure to always do this in a subtle and professional manner. Finally, since he is, after all, your manager, there will be times you will have to conform.

Take Note Of Your Manager's Style
No two managers are the same, so it is important to understand what makes your manager tick. Try to learn what you can to find out what your manager expects and how you can succeed under his leadership. Find out what your manager's professional background is and how your manager reached his position. Take note of your manager's work habits, such as the hours he works. All of this will give you clues to how you will best be able to work with each other so you can both gain the most from your relationship.

Subtly, Test Your Manager's Limits
In an always subtle and professional manner, periodically test your manager's limits by experimentation. This means, see what you can and cannot get away with. Be aware: this does not mean see what you can and cannot do wrong. You should never look to do anything wrong. Just see what your manager's expectations are regarding certain issues. For example, if you like to take your one-hour lunch break at noon, but he wants to meet with you regularly for a half-hour at noon, you will have to adjust.

Conform At Times

As in the last example, there are certain times when you will have to conform to your manager's expectations. After all, he is your manager, and that means he is your boss. There may be situations, however, where you can work out a compromise. Remember that your manager was once a subordinate and most likely still has a manager, plus he is a human being, so you can usually talk things out in times of uncertainty.

Examples

Kate joined a company after several years of experience at another job. As soon as she began working with her new manager, she realized they did not think alike. Her new manager had some suggestions for her, and he asked her to conform to his and the company's standards regarding certain issues. She refused, since she had been doing things her own way for a long time. Therefore, the two fought about everything. Her manager won the final battle as Kate was abruptly fired.

Don worked for the same manager as Kate. He also realized his work habits were unlike his manager's. Therefore, he soon figured out the areas where they did not see eye to eye. He tried things out his way to see how his manager reacted to them. Some of the things his manager did not care much about. Others he did, and those were the areas where Don had to conform. Don was successful in managing his manager.

"Learn to adjust yourself to the conditions you have to endure, but make a point of trying to alter or correct conditions so that they are most favorable to you." – William Frederick Book, author.

22. Expand Your Horizons

The surest way to expand your horizons at work is to always accept additional responsibility when you are presented with the opportunity to do so. First, it will show you have ambition. Second, the more responsibility you take on, the greater exposure you will receive within your company. This added exposure could help put you on a fast track to become a rising star at work.

Always Accept More Responsibility
Some people are afraid of accepting additional responsibility at work because of the extra pressures and stresses it may bring. This is fine for those who do not want to progress, but for the ambitious ones who do, always accept more responsibility. Although it may, indeed, include a few added headaches, it will also test your ability to set yourself apart from the rest of your coworkers.

With Responsibility Comes Exposure
There is a direct correlation between the amount of responsibility you have at work to the level of exposure you will receive within your company. The more responsibility you have, the greater exposure you will receive, and the more likely you will come into contact with upper management in your company. The less responsibility you have, the less exposure you will receive, and the less likely you will come into contact with upper management in your company.

Exposure Will Help You Rise To The Top
If your desire is to stay in the same position, you do not have to be concerned with the amount of exposure you will receive within your company. On the other hand, if your goal is to rise up the ranks to reach the top, there is nothing as beneficial to you as a high level of exposure. Upper man-

agement is often eager to have their most ambitious employees join them to help their company thrive.

Examples

George was a gentleman who had been in the same position at the same company for many years. Over time, he had become proficient at his job, so he was often presented with opportunities to expand his horizons and take on additional responsibility. He never accepted, however, because he felt comfortable with what he was doing and did not want to bear any greater burden. Therefore, George occupied the same position for several more years as he watched numerous, far less experienced, employees pass him by.

Penny began her career a short time after George in a similar position with a smaller company. Unlike George, however, Penny was ambitious and constantly sought and accepted greater responsibility. Upper management soon realized she was a diamond in the rough, and she was promoted in rapid succession. Consequently, she gained an outstanding reputation in her industry and was courted by other suitors. Penny was then hired by George's company and ran the department he worked in.

"Unless you try to do something beyond what you have mastered, you will never grow." – C. R. Lawton

23. Remember Where You Came From

When you reach the top of your company, always remember where you came from. This is something many people at the bottom say they will do if and when they ever get to the top, but these same people often seem to forget this once they climb to the top. It is important to remind yourself that you were not always at the top of the heap, so do not go on a power trip once you get there. As a manager, it is usually helpful to remember the qualities you liked and disliked in your managers.

<u>You Were Not Always At The Top</u>
Remembering where you came from simply means keeping in mind that you were not always at the top of your company. You had to begin your career somewhere. Chances are, you began at an entry-level position just as many of your current subordinates, and you had to scratch and claw your way to the top just as most of them are trying to do now.

<u>Do Not Go On A Power Trip</u>
Sometimes it is easy to reach the top of your company and, all of a sudden, develop a big head. You let your ego get the best of you and begin to think you are too big for your britches. You start to feel you are too good for everyone else you work with because of your job title. This is what is known as going on a power trip. You must take great pains to not let this happen to you, because it can be severely damaging to you, your subordinates, your career, and your company.

<u>Recall The Qualities You Liked/Disliked In Your Managers</u>
One of the simplest, yet most effective, ways to become a successful manager is to recall the qualities you liked and disliked in your managers, and manage your subordinates accordingly. Take all of the positive traits your former man-

agers had and try to mold them into your personality to make them work for you. If you appreciated and responded to them, chances are your subordinates will, too. Similarly, take all of the negative characteristics your managers had and make it a point not to imitate them.

Examples
Karen began her career at the bottom of a large company, and after years of hard work, she earned a management position. Along the way, she had some good managers as well as a few bad ones. When she started managing, she used this as a time to treat her subordinates the way some of her bad managers treated her in order to gain some form of payback. Her subordinates rebelled, and Karen's power trip was a short one.

Bill charted his way along a similar path as Karen at a different company. He also experienced several managers he liked working with as well as a handful of others he did not. He always had his eye on a management position and worked quite feverishly to get there. He consciously tried to take note of what to do from his better managers, as well as what not to do from his worse managers. As a result, Bill became a standout manager and quickly rose to the top.

**"Some people grow under responsibility, others merely swell." –
Cedric Hubbell Whitman (1916-1979), American classicist and poet.**

24. Treat Subordinates With Respect

A manager should always treat her subordinates with respect. Remember, as a manager, you were in their position at one time, and they may be in your position some day. Therefore, try to learn from the past and be a positive role model for the future. In addition, if you treat your subordinates with respect, you will earn their respect. Finally, the respect you give to your subordinates will be their greatest motivation to succeed.

<u>You Were Them, And Eventually, They May Be You</u>
When you were a subordinate, you most likely used your managers' behavior as examples of certain things you would want to do, as well as other things you would not want to do, if and when you were in their position. Similarly, your subordinates will probably utilize parts of your management style for the same purpose. Set a good example by treating your subordinates with respect, and when it is their turn to manage, chances are, they will do the same for others.

<u>You Treat Them With Respect, You Will Earn Their Respect</u>
If you treat others with respect, you will earn their respect. It is that simple. Everyone at work, no matter what position they are in, deserves respect. Just because you are a manager and you have people working for you, does not mean you have any right to treat them with any less respect than you would like for them to give you. If you do, you will never earn the respect of your subordinates.

<u>Your Respect Will Be Their Greatest Motivation</u>
The most successful managers know how to motivate people. Nothing motivates subordinates more than their manager's respect. If you treat your subordinates with respect, you will motivate them, and they will be happy workers. Happy workers will do everything they can to perform their jobs

well. If your subordinates perform their jobs well, they will make you appear to be a great manager.

Examples

Annie was an intelligent, dedicated, and demanding woman who worked diligently and became a manager in her company at a relatively young age. When she did, however, she set a poor example by treating her subordinates with a lack of respect. As a result, her subordinates had no respect for her, grew increasingly unhappy, and their job performance suffered. This, of course, reflected poorly on the once bright star, Annie, and her skyward progression was soon altered.

It took Misa much longer than Annie to reach the management level in the same company, but when she finally became a manager, she had a burning desire to be a good one. She also wanted to serve as a positive role model for her subordinates. Therefore, she treated them with respect and, in turn, earned their respect. Her subordinates were motivated and happy, and this was reflected in their productivity. Misa became one of the best, and most respected, managers in her company.

"When I was coaching, the one thought that I would try to get across to my players was that everything I do each day, everything I say, I must first think what effect it will have on everyone concerned." – Frank Layden, former National Basketball Association coach and president of the Utah Jazz.

25. Do Not Yell At Others

Similar to Tom Hanks' line "there is no crying in baseball" from the movie "A League of Their Own," there is no yell-ing in the workplace. There are no ifs, ands, or buts about it. Never yell at anyone on the job, no matter who you or they are, or what they do. Nobody has any right to do so. Aside from being wrong, if you yell at someone, it will reduce that person's motivation, and it will make you look foolish.

You Do Not Have The Right To Yell At Others

Just because you are the boss and are managing others, you do not have the right to raise your voice and yell at people. It is inappropriate regardless of the situation, and there are much more professional alternatives. For example, if you are upset with one of your subordinates, sit down with him and have a person-to-person discussion to clear the air. It should never get more heated than that.

Reduces Motivation

Aside from yelling at others on the job being inappropriate, it is also unproductive. If a manager yells at a subordinate, it will reduce the employee's motivation. That will not get the manager, the subordinate, or the company anywhere. In-stead, if a manager addresses a subordinate with a calm and cool demeanor, it will keep that worker motivated, which can only have a positive impact on everyone involved and keep the company moving in the right direction.

Makes You Look Foolish

In addition to yelling being unprofessional and potentially damaging all the way around, in the most basic terms, it will make you look foolish. It will not make the person you are yelling at look foolish, but it will make *you* appear that way. A fool is the last thing you want to be labeled in your com-pany. A manager yelling at a subordinate, or anyone yelling at anyone at work, creates an embarrassing situation and ultimately makes the person yelling seem foolish.

Examples
Jarrod joined his company and worked hard for many years to become a manager. Once he became a manager, he seemed to think he had the right to yell at his subordinates. This obviously upset, angered, and deflated those on the receiving end of his yelling, but it also disturbed other managers who despised his behavior. More than once, several of these managers sat down with him to set him straight. Jarrod continued his foolish behavior, however, and his job was quickly terminated.

Kurt dutifully climbed the same corporate ladder Jarrod did to reach a management position, but he seemed to stay on a somewhat even keel no matter the circumstance. Even when he was angry with his subordinates, he never considered yelling at them. He knew that would be improper as well as unproductive. Instead, he addressed these instances in a professional manner. Kurt's subordinates remained motivated and he stayed in a high-level management position.

"Nothing lowers the level on conversation more than raising the voice." – Stanley Horowitz

26. Delegate Whenever You Can

A manager should try to delegate responsibility to her subordinates whenever possible. Delegating is the process of entrusting others under your supervision to get work done that you are ultimately responsible for. Delegating is the most efficient manner of completing tasks. It also allows you to utilize your management ability to the fullest extent, and it helps you empower your subordinates.

<u>The Most Efficient Way To Get Things Done</u>
Delegating is efficient because it allows you to complete many assignments simultaneously. For example, if you have five projects to complete, instead of only *you* attending to all of the details, ultimately, you can delegate each project to a different subordinate. You can oversee their work, and the tasks will inevitably be finished in a timely manner.

<u>Allows You To Manage To The Fullest Extent</u>
A big part of managing is teaching. In the previous example, if it is just you working on all five projects, the learning is limited. If you delegate the work to different subordinates, however, all of them will be learning under your tutelage. The benefits of teaching go well beyond these five assignments. Once your subordinates have learned how to complete these tasks, when similar tasks surface in the future, your staff will be able to handle them more readily. This is managing to the fullest extent.

<u>Empowers Your Subordinates</u>
Once again, referring to the previous example, if you are the only person working on all five projects, your subordinates will either be watching you or not doing anything. They will become bored, feel unwanted, unneeded, and unimportant. On the other hand, if you delegate the five assignments to them, they will feel empowered, and it will help them grow

as employees. They will also gain confidence and will be a greater asset to you in the future. Finally, it will make you and your company more productive in the long term.

Examples

Monique was a smart, energetic, and hardworking young woman who quickly rose to the management level in her company. As a manager, however, her work was not getting done efficiently. Since she was used to completing all of her assignments on her own, she had a difficult time delegating any of her now greater workload. As a result, her subordinates began feeling frustrated. Monique never overcame this problem, and she did not progress beyond her initial management role.

Joseph was a manager in the same company as Monique. When he initially reached the management level, he felt a bit overwhelmed by all of the work. He quickly discovered that by delegating, however, he could get more projects done in far less time and with much greater accuracy. Plus, it helped him refine his management skills, and it made his subordinates feel more valuable. Not only did Joseph rise well beyond his first management title, but the majority of his subordinates prospered in his company as well.

"Delegating means letting others become the experts and hence the best." – Timothy W. Firnstahl, restauranteur and writer.

27. How To Evaluate Others

Evaluating others in the workplace is not a process that should be taken lightly. Evaluations should be performed regularly with an aim to help employees maximize their job skills. Executed correctly, evaluations will not only help those being evaluated, but they will benefit their managers and the overall company as well. Managers should begin evaluations by praising their subordinates' strengths, then identifying ways they can improve, and finally, helping them chart their career course.

Praise What They Are Doing Well
In order to get employee evaluations off on the right foot, it is critical for managers to begin by praising their subordinates in the areas they are doing well. It is rare that employees do not have at least one strong suit, and by starting with strengths, your employees will feel appreciated and know that you are trying to be fair. It will also allow your forthcoming improvement areas and suggestions to be more palatable.

Let Them Know How They Can Improve
Just as it is rare that employees do not have at least one strong point, it is uncommon for them to not have at least one area where they can improve. Areas of improvement should always be communicated to subordinates along with suggestions from their manager on how they may become better. It is also important to point out that if an area of improvement is actually a glaring weakness, a formal evaluation is not the first time an employee should be made aware of this.

Help Them Chart Their Course
The final step in the evaluation process should be for managers to help their subordinates chart their career course. First,

let them know where the progress they make in their current position could eventually lead them. Then, confirm that this is in sync with their career aspirations. This process will help them see that all of the hard work they are putting in today could lead to a bright future tomorrow, which will serve to motivate them to reach their full potential.

Examples

Connie was a busy manager in her company. When it came time to do her employee evaluations, they were often done late because they were obviously not among her top priorities. When she did get around to doing evaluations, she focused solely on her subordinates' weaknesses with few suggestions on how they could improve. Since there were no positive or career growth aspects to them, her subordinates felt unappreciated. Therefore, their work suffered, and so did Connie's management career.

Cindy was a thoughtful, considerate, and fair-minded manager in the same company as Connie. She realized the importance of employee evaluations, and she tried to get them completed in a consistent and timely manner. She used evaluations to make her subordinates feel proud of the good work they had done and to focus on ways to improve in their jobs and grow in their careers. This helped Cindy's management career blossom as well.

"To say 'well done' to any bit of good work is to take hold of the powers which have made the effort and strengthen them beyond our knowledge." – Phillips Brooks (1835-1893), American Protestant Episcopal clergyman.

Part IV – Ready–Set–Go – Take Action

28. Honesty Is The Best Policy

When you were a child, you probably learned from your parents that in life, honesty is the best policy. This was sound advice as it applies to the workplace, too. Always be honest when you are dealing with others on your job. If you are not, you will develop a bad reputation, and nobody will want to work with or for you. Remember that lies will always come back to haunt you.

Always Be Honest
The reputation you develop early on at work will stick with you throughout your career. Above all else, if you establish yourself as an honest person, this is the reputation you will carry with you. If you prove to be dishonest, however, this is how you will be perceived. If you want to have a successful career, always be honest. No matter what happens, there is no excuse or reason to be any other way.

Nobody Wants To Work With Or For A Dishonest Person
If you are an honest person at work, people will know it, and they will be attracted to the prospect of working with or for you. It will also be the foundation for building solid working relationships with your coworkers. On the other hand, if you are perceived as a dishonest person, nobody will want to work with or for you, and you will have major problems earning your coworkers' trust.

Lies Will Always Come Back To Haunt You
If you tell a lie at work, it will inevitably come back to haunt you sometime in your career. You may think you can get away with it, and that it may even help you, in the short term. Most likely it will not, but even if it does, you will pay the price for it in the long run. In addition, once you lie, you

will probably have to lie again to cover up your original lie. In essence, lies often take on a snowball effect. To avoid this mess, you should not lie even once.

Examples

Kendra was an intelligent, ambitious, and cunning young woman who was quickly promoted into a management role in her company. Her coworkers were often impressed, but somewhat suspicious of the crafty methods she had of getting her work done. Initially, Kendra was productive, so nobody questioned her. Eventually it was discovered, however, that many of her results were based on lies and deceit that then came back to haunt her. Kendra's reputation was destroyed and she was soon fired.

Vera was a smart, sincere, and dedicated employee in the same company as Kendra. Her coworkers enjoyed working with her, and they trusted her because of her honesty. Through a combination of hard work and a stellar reputation, she was promoted to a management position. Vera maintained her integrity, and she quickly became one of her company's most popular and productive managers.

"Honesty is the single most important factor having a direct bearing on the final success of an individual, corporation, or product." – Ed McMahon, announcer, television host, and actor.

29. Never Complain

Never complain to anyone at work. This does not mean do not speak your mind and express your feelings about matters that bother you. To the contrary, it is important you do this whenever you feel the need. Do not do it in a complaining and whining manner, however, because that will get you nowhere. In addition, complaining is contagious, and constant complaining will give you a bad reputation.

Complaining Will Get You Nowhere
If you do not feel good about something happening at work, complaining and whining about it to your coworkers will get you nowhere. The way to handle a situation such as this is to calmly and rationally gather your thoughts on the matter, figure out who can help you improve the condition, and then address it directly with that person. Together, try to arrive at a resolution.

Complaining Is Contagious
If something is bothering you and you complain about it to your coworkers, the same thing will probably begin to bother them. In a matter of time, you will have an office full of employees who will be unhappy and complaining. This will be harmful to you, your coworkers, and your entire company's morale. Stop the bleeding before it spreads by not complaining because complaining is contagious.

Constant Complaining Will Give You A Bad Reputation
Just as you do not want to develop a reputation for being dishonest, you do not want to be labeled a complainer. If you become known as a complainer, your coworkers will avoid you, because they will not want you to bring them down with you. If you do continue to complain, you may be escorted to the exit door, and your reputation will follow you throughout your career.

Examples
Gus was a corporate veteran who obtained a new job after many years of working at another firm. He had a difficult time accepting his new company's philosophy and structure. As a result, he constantly complained to his coworkers, and they did not enjoy working with him. In addition, his managers feared his constant complaining would rub off on others and hurt employee morale. Therefore, Gus was forced to find another new job.

Jim also gained his experience elsewhere before joining the same company as Gus. He, too, had some reservations about the way things were done at his new place of work, but he constructively directed his concerns to his managers. Together, they arrived at solutions and compromise. He quickly developed a reputation for being levelheaded, open-minded, and easy to work with. Things worked out well for Jim in this company as he began to fit in and feel comfortable.

"The tendency to whining and complaining may be taken as the surest sign symptom of little souls and inferior intellects." – Lord Jeffrey (Jeffrey Francis, 1773-1850), Scottish literary critic and jurist.

30. Certain Topics Are A No-No

Certain topics should never be discussed, or even alluded to, in the workplace. These include subjects that, at best, people may take offense to and, at worst, may result in legal action or, quite possibly, violence. First, do not talk about anyone's race, creed, or color. Second, do not make any sexual connotations. Finally, do not get too personal with anyone.

Do Not Talk About Anyone's Race, Creed, Or Color
At work, the topic of anyone's race, creed, or color should not be discussed, and it should never be the basis for any decisions made regarding anything. If you broach this subject, even if what you say is not meant to be harmful or hurtful, it may easily be taken out of context or received the wrong way. If it is, you will be known as a bigot, and you will put yourself in a position to be sued by your victim and fired by your employer.

Do Not Make Any Sexual Connotations
Do not make any sexual connotations on the job. Just as anyone's race, creed, or color should never be an issue, the same applies to anyone's sexual orientation. Exercise extreme caution when touching coworkers in what can be perceived as the wrong way or place. In addition, be careful about any comments you make. Once again, if you make remarks you intend to be of an innocent nature, they may not be taken as such by a coworker.

Do Not Get Too Personal With Anyone
It is not a good idea to get too personal with anyone at work. This is not to say you should never attempt to become friends with your coworkers, because you may want to extend some interoffice relationships to the outside, and that is fine. It also does not imply that romantic connections should never result from people working together. It just means be

cautious and smart about how quickly, how much, and with whom you interact on a personal level at your job.

Examples

Barbara was a bright and talented woman who was in a position of authority at her company. She had several people reporting to her, including both men and women. Barbara often made comments to a couple of her male subordinates about how attractive she thought they were. In time, her remarks became worse, with sexual overtones. As a result, these two men felt uncomfortable, and after a while, they began to complain. Barbara was soon fired.

Keith was an employee in the same company as Barbara. Actually, he was one of her subordinates she had targeted, and who later complained about her comments. Because he knew how it felt to be a victim of these sexual innuendoes, he went out of his way, and was extra careful not to do the same to his female coworkers. Keith learned from his experience and helped others learn to avoid being on either end of this issue.

"The unspoken word never does harm." – Lajos Kossuth (1802-1894), Hungarian revolutionary leader.

31. Dress For Success

Over the last several years, many companies' dress require-
ments have gone from formal to casual. Even so, now just as
before, it is important to dress for success. Dressing for success means always looking the part. If you are expected to
dress a certain way for your job, dress that way. Just make
sure you look good because when you look good you feel
good. If you are ever unsure about how to dress, ask for advice from someone who may know.

Always Look The Part
Even today, some companies still expect employees to dress
formally by wearing a suit, or at least a jacket and a tie.
Others allow for dress to be business-casual, and there are
varying degrees of that definition. Some jobs have no dress
code at all, yet others require a specific uniform. Whichever
category your company falls into, it is always important for
you to look the part. Whatever you are supposed to wear to
work, wear it well and with pride.

When You Look Good You Feel Good
When the phrase, "when you look good you feel good,"
gained popularity on Saturday Night Live, it generated a lot
of laughs, but it is an absolutely true statement. If you clean
yourself up, dress right, and are comfortable with the way
you look, you will, no doubt, feel good about yourself. If
you feel good about yourself, you will perform better at your
job, and vice versa.

When Unsure How To Dress, Ask
There will inevitably be situations and special occasions
when you will be unsure about how to dress for work. When
these instances occur, do not just take a guess at what may be
appropriate. If you do, there will be a chance you will be
wrong and not look the part for your job. Instead, do not be

afraid to ask someone, such as your manager, who will be able to let you know. Chances are, you may save yourself a lot of regret, and maybe even some embarrassment, later on.

Examples
Dean was a humorous, free-spirited young man who began rising up the ranks in his large company. After years of re-quiring its employees to dress formally, his firm initiated a casual dress policy for Fridays. The first Friday this started, Dean came to work in ripped jeans, sneakers, and a tee shirt. His manager immediately took him aside, reprimanded him for taking advantage of his company's new rule, and sent him home to change. Dean's manager never forgot this, and it stalled his progress.

Tim was employed by the same company and at the same time as Dean. When the decision to institute casual Fridays was announced, he was unsure exactly what this meant. Therefore, he went into his manager's office and asked for clarification of the new dress code. His manager explained they were expected to dress in a business-casual manner, which according to the company's definition meant no jeans, sneakers, or tee shirts. This helped Tim dress the proper way, and he had no problems from there.

"Good clothes open all doors." – Thomas Fuller (1608-1661), English clergyman and author.

32. Arrive On Time

Do everything you can to arrive on time every day of work. This way, you will always start your day on the right foot. Never get in the habit of being late. Always give an honest day's work for an honest day's pay. Consistently getting to work on time will show you are reliable. In addition, you will never miss out on any opportunities that you might miss if you arrive to work late.

Give An Honest Day's Work For An Honest Day's Pay
The most fundamental reason to always get to work on time is that it is what you are being paid to do. If your official workday begins at nine o'clock in the morning, you should never arrive later than that time. Of course, there may be unavoidable circumstances from time to time that may force you to be late. First, these should be the exception, not the rule. Second, if this does happen, be sure to call your manager or one of your coworkers to let them know your situation and when they can expect you to be in.

Shows You Are Reliable
A positive outcome of always arriving to work on time is that timeliness will show that you are conscientious and reliable. It will be an indicator to your manager that you can be counted on when she needs you most. On the other hand, if you consistently get to work late, your manager will take that as a reflection of your character and your work ethic. Then, she will not be able to trust that you will be there for her at crunch time.

Do Not Want To Miss Out On Any Opportunities
An important reason from a career standpoint to always get to work on time is that you do not want to miss out on any opportunities. For example, if you get an urgent phone call first thing in the morning and you are not at your desk be-

cause you are late, it could be a missed opportunity for business. Or, if your manager is trying to find one of her subordinates to handle a high profile assignment and you are not in the office, she will probably search for one of your co-workers to take care of it instead.

Examples

Didi was an intelligent and brazen young woman who worked at a small company. She was good at all aspects of her job except she had a bad habit of arriving to work late just about every day. Her usual excuse was that she was not a morning person, so she could not help it. This posed a problem for her manager because Didi was often not around when important business calls came in for her. This hurt the bottom line of her small company, so Didi was let go.

Petra was a focused and dedicated woman who held a similar position to Didi in a different small firm. She was diligent about getting to work on time because she cared a lot about her job. Without fail, she was always there when her manager needed her and was often in the right place at the right time for plum assignments. As a result, Petra excelled in her career and quickly rose to the top of her small company.

"Promptitude is not only a duty, but is also a part of good manners; it is favorable to fortune, reputation, influence, and usefulness; a little attention and energy will form the habit, so as to make it easy and delightful." – Charles Simmons

33. Prioritize And Juggle

The most efficient and effective ways to maximize your job production are to develop the abilities to prioritize your work and juggle your assignments. This means: know which parts of your workload are most and least important, and have more than one project going on simultaneously. If you can develop these abilities, they will help you become organized and show your versatility. This will increase your value to your company.

Helps You Become Organized
If you can prioritize your workload, it will help you become organized. To accomplish this, maintain a list of tasks you need to complete in order of their importance and deadlines. Consistently revise, update, and refer to this list to make sure you are always aware of what needs to get done and by when. If you are ever unsure about a specific task's level of importance or deadline, ask your manager.

Shows You Are Versatile
Once you have your priorities in order, the ability to juggle your assignments will show you are versatile. Juggling your assignments is accepting, and being able to concentrate on, more than one project at one time. Therefore, if your manager asks you to help him with a specific task, instead of saying no because you are working on something else, accept it and juggle it with the rest of your workload.

Increases Your Value
If you can prioritize your work and juggle your assignments, you will prove to be an organized and versatile employee. An organized and versatile employee is a valuable one. A company will go out of its way to keep a valuable employee happy. Keep in mind, prioritizing and juggling are abilities

that can be learned and will get better with practice. They are definitely worth the effort.

Examples

Marv was a warm, friendly, and laid-back young man when he joined his large company. He was immediately over-whelmed by the fast-paced and demanding environment. He was given several tasks to complete early on, and he had trouble knowing which ones to do first and how to get them all done in time. He did not ask anyone, so as more and more work piled on his desk, his situation grew worse. He dug himself into such a deep hole, he was unable to get out. Marv's job did not last long.

Gayle was a bright, talented, and ambitious young woman who entered into the same large company as Marv. Initially, she was also a bit taken aback by the fever-pitched atmos-phere, but she challenged herself to prioritize her work and juggle her assignments, so she could get everything done in a timely manner. When she was unsure about how to proceed at any given point, she asked her manager. With this atti-tude, it did not take Gayle long to thrive and become an in-valuable employee.

"It is the mark of great people to treat trifles as trifles and important matters as important." – Doris May Lessing (1919-), British novelist and short-story writer.

34. Double Check Everything

After everything you do at work, before anyone else can see it, double check it to make sure it is correct. This way, you will decrease your margin for error by catching any mistakes you may have made before anyone else can. By producing more work with fewer mistakes, it will show you pay attention to detail. It will also indicate to your manager that you will require less supervision in the future.

Decreases Your Margin For Error
If you take time to recheck your work, you will decrease your margin for error. If you decrease your margin for error, you will save yourself, your manager, and your company time and money in the long run. The fewer mistakes you make that your manager has to catch the quicker you and your manager will have to move on and focus on other things. The more mistakes you make that your manager has to catch the more time it will take for both of you. In business, time is money.

Shows You Pay Attention To Detail
If you double check everything thereby producing more work with fewer mistakes, it will show you pay attention to detail. If you show you pay attention to detail, it will show you handle your work with care. If you do not recheck everything, you will invariably turn in work containing more mistakes. This will show you are careless, and companies have no room for careless workers. Those who pay attention to detail, however, are always in demand.

You Will Require Less Supervision
Another byproduct of producing more work with fewer mistakes is your manager will have greater faith in you, and you will require less supervision in the future. Then, if you can continue to churn out work with relatively few mistakes

without needing your manager's supervision, you will put yourself in an excellent position to be promoted. Remember that this all begins with double checking everything.

Examples
Judy was an eager-to-please young woman who started working for her company right out of college. She was given a few tasks to complete during her first few weeks on the job. She tried too hard to impress her manager by finishing her assignments quickly, so she made numerous careless mistakes. Therefore, her manager had to take time to point out her errors and review them with her. Despite her manager's best efforts, her careless mistakes kept coming. Judy did not last long in this position.

Melanie was assigned a similar workload as Judy after she joined the same company upon her graduation. She wanted to make sure the work she turned in was as accurate as possible, so she consistently made sure to double check. Although this took additional time, especially in the beginning, she knew it would be worth it in the long run. Whenever her manager went over her assignments, he was impressed by her few errors. Melanie continued to minimize her mistakes and quickly earned a promotion.

"The difference between failure and success is doing a thing nearly right and doing it exactly right." – Edward Simmons

35. A Time For Work And A Time For Play

In order to maintain a successful career and personal life, it is mandatory to be able to separate the two. There is a time for work, and there is a time for play. When you are at work, you are on your company's time, so give them one hundred percent of your time and attention. When you are on your time, have fun, and try not to bring work home with you. In order to get the most out of both your career and your personal life, try to develop a work hard, play hard attitude.

<u>When You Are On Their Time, Give Them Your Time</u>
From the time you arrive at your office until the time you walk outside the door at the end of each day, excluding your typical lunch break, you are on your company's time. Therefore, never fail to show your total dedication and commitment by doing everything in your power to get your job done to the best of your ability. After all, this is what you are being paid for. Anything less, you will be cheating your company and ultimately yourself.

<u>When You Are On Your Time, Have Fun!</u>
Before you arrive at your office, after you walk outside the door at the end of each day, and even during your lunch break, have fun! When it comes right down to it, that is what life is all about. It is also what you work for – to have the time and money to enjoy yourself, your family, and friends, as well as your activities, hobbies, and interests. Try not to bring work home with you either mentally or physically. Although there will probably be times you will have to, do everything you can to keep them to a minimum.

<u>Bottom Line – Work Hard And Play Hard!</u>
The bottom line is to strive to develop a work hard, play hard attitude and lifestyle. By doing this, you will make the most out of every day of your career and your life. It does not get

any better than that. In essence, the two feed off each other. The more fulfilled you are in your career, the more you will be able to enjoy your personal life. The happier you are in your personal life, the more successful you will be in your career.

Examples

Ross was an intellectual and dedicated manager in a large company. He was great at his job, but his personal life suffered as a result. He had a difficult time separating the two. Even on his own time, he was constantly thinking about his work. He routinely clocked in long hours and brought work home with him on a regular basis. After several years of this, Ross burned out, his career suffered, and he was left with not much of a personal life.

Dana was a smart woman who was a manager in the same company as Ross. She worked diligently and was focused when she was in the office, too. With the rewards from her successful career, however, she enjoyed a fulfilling personal life with her family and friends. She adopted a work hard, play hard attitude early on, and it served her well. Dana spearheaded to the top and continued to have a blast!

**"If you want creative workers, give them enough time to play." –
John Cleese, comic actor and writer.**

36. Take Breaks And Vacations To Avoid Burnout

To help you stay healthy and avoid burnout, take breaks and vacations. You earn and deserve them. Breaks should be taken occasionally, and be kept brief, in order to help you maintain your focus throughout the day. Vacation time should be taken advantage of to the fullest extent in order to keep you going throughout the year. Overall, it is imperative to strive to achieve a well-balanced lifestyle.

Occasionally Take Brief Breaks To Maintain Your Focus
Breaks during the workday are traditionally unofficial and subjective. In other words, there are usually no blocks of time set out for you to take them. If once or twice a day you feel the need to take a five-minute break to clear your head, however, you should do so by either getting a cup of coffee, taking a walk, getting some fresh air, or anything else to that effect. You will, no doubt, come back feeling rejuvenated and be able to better maintain your focus.

Take Advantage Of Your Vacation Time – You Earned It!
In the United States, over the course of a year, it is common to earn between two and five weeks vacation time. The amount of your time is normally dependent upon your length of service at your company. Whatever time you earn, the time is yours to take as you wish. Nobody should ever make you feel guilty about taking off any time that is yours. Occasionally, your manager may request you do not schedule your vacation during a busy work period. That is fine, as long as you eventually get to take all of your time.

Strive For A Well-Balanced Lifestyle
In the end, it all comes down to achieving a well-balanced lifestyle. This is what everyone seems to be striving for. Everyone wants to have a successful career, healthy and happy family, lots of friends, and the time and money to en-

joy all the pleasantries life has to offer. There is no reason you cannot have all of this. Just keep working smart and you will succeed. Of course, be sure to have fun along the way!

Example

If you notice, unlike the previous thirty-five "Examples" sections, this heading reads "Example." There will only be one of them, ideally a positive one. The example will be you, the reader. It will be left for you to fill in. It does not have to be done right away, unless you feel you have already achieved a well-balanced lifestyle. You may have, and if you have, congratulations! It is quite an accomplishment, and it is something to be proud of. If you have not yet achieved this, however, you are similar to many still striving, and eventually you will. Try to take some of the lessons and examples from this book, and use them to help you along your journey. Wherever you are in the course of your career and your life, good luck, and remember to work smart and succeed!

"Every man who possibly can should force himself to a holiday of a full month in a year, whether he feels like taking it or not." – William James (1842-1910), American psychologist and philosopher.